THE
HEAVENLY
FOOTMAN

THE
HEAVENLY
FOOTMAN

A Puritan's View

of

how to get to Heaven

John Bunyan

Introduced by J.I. Packer

Christian Heritage

ISBN 1 85792 667 6

Introduction © J.I. Packer

© Christian Focus Publications

Published 2002 by
Christian Focus Publications,
Geanies House, Fearn, Ross-shire,
IV20 1TW, Great Britain

www.christianfocus.com

Cover design by Alister MacInnes

Printed by Cox & Wyman Ltd, Reading, Berkshire

Contents

Introduction
J.I.Packer

In the pre-photography world of the seventeenth century, persons of quality by birth and persons of distinction for their achievements were regularly painted, drawn, or engraved by professional artists. Artists, willy-nilly, being the imaginative people they are, interpret their subjects differently, picturing what they think they see as they look at them, so that portraits of the same person may vary in striking ways. So it is with the two surviving likenesses of Bunyan. That by Thomas Sadler, which hangs in London's National Portrait Gallery, shows him as he was in 1685, at the age of 56. He is dressed for the pulpit, has a Bible in his hand, and looks very serious, purposeful and under tension; indeed, he is almost scowling. You feel this is

Bunyan the Lord's messenger, looking at you in preparation for preaching to you in an applicatory and admonitory way. But there is also a pencil study of Bunyan from the same period by Robert White, who we are told had a flair for sympathetic portraiture. White's Bunyan, like Sadler's, looks at us, but in quite a different way: he is relaxed, genial, faintly smiling yet somewhat withdrawn, as man (you would say) with a great deal of inner life, at peace in himself, and ready to share what he sees and knows.

Both date from the days when *Pilgrim's Progress* had catapulted its author into stardom. Maybe White made Bunyan too handsome while Sadler made him too rugged; yet there is truth in both ways of seeing him. His homiletic writings really are tense and fierce, and no doubt his preaching was the same; while *Pilgrim's Progress*, and other writings in the same allegorical and parabolic vein, reveal whimsy and wit, and are sometimes downright comic. These are the two sides of John Bunyan, a faithful minister and a fascinating man.

By birth he was not a person of quality; just the reverse. He was the son of a brazier whose family had come down in the world and who now ran a metalworker's shop in Elstow, a village of 69 cottages outside the town of Bedford. He was sent to school to learn to read and write, but was soon withdrawn so that he could learn his father's trade. No doubt the plan was that he should work in the shop permanently. In 1644, however, when he was sixteen, his mother and sister died, his father remarried, and he himself was drafted for a two-and-a-half year stint in the Parliamentary army. It is not perhaps surprising that when he got back to Elstow, a 'veteran' (as today's

Americans would say) still in his teens, rather than settle down in the shop he struck out for independence; he became a tinker (that is, a metalworking itinerant), launched himself into poverty by marriage, and so continued till he was gaoled in 1660. Tinkers, being itinerants and thus potential getaway artists, were thought of as rascals, like shepherds in Jesus' day and tramps in ours, and the tinkering trade was not one that would make a man rich. It was hardly an auspicious beginning to Bunyan's career.

But by the end of his life he was a celebrity. He was an established Christian writer, whose *Pilgrim's Progress* was a runaway best-seller; he was a popular preacher, who drew crowds of thousands in London and of hundreds when he preached in Bedford, where he now pastored a church, and in the villages around; he was a friend of the great John Owen, who told Charles II that he would gladly give all his learning to be able to preach with Bunyan's power; he was called 'Bishop Bunyan' behind his back; and he sat for two of the top artists of his day. He had, as we would say, arrived.

The story of the progress of this pilgrim divides neatly into three periods, thus:

(1) The years 1648–60 were Bunyan's time of discovery. First, over a five-year period of soul-shaking ups and downs, which he later chronicled for the encouraging of his own converts in *Grace Abounding to the Chief of Sinners*, he found peace with God. His spiritual quest began when he married a godly man's daughter whose dowry consisted of two Puritan works, Arthur Dent's *Plain Man's Pathway to Heaven* and Lewis Bayley's

Practice of Piety. He started attending church; stopped swearing, dancing, and acting up; read the Bible; met some poor born-again women from a new church in Bradford and came to know John Gifford, their pastor; became Christ-centred and cross-centred through reading Luther on Galatians; spent two years fearing he had committed the unpardonable sin of abandoning Christ; and finally, in 1653, was baptized by Gifford in the river Ouse as a credible convert.

Then, second, he found he had a gift for pulpit ministry. Having gone as a trainee with members of the Bedford church who preached in the villages, and having testified and exhorted in small groups, Bunyan was formally instated as a lay preacher in 1656, and from then on fulfilled his own village ministry with much acceptance. His emphasis was constantly evangelistic: 'I found my spirit leaned most after awakening and converting work.'

Third, he found he had a gift for writing popular Christian literature. He began with polemics: *Some Gospel Truths Opened* (1656) and *A Vindication of . . . Some Gospel-Truths Opened* (1657) were against Quakerism. *A Few Sighs from Hell* (1658) and *The Doctrine of the Law and Grace Unfolded* (1659) came next. Articulate and a fast worker, with remarkable natural powers of analysis and argument, Bunyan never looked back from this beginning; he wrote and wrote, and by the end of his life had produced sixty treatises of different sizes, amounting in all to something like two million words.

(2) The years 1660–72 were Bunyan's time of dishonour, when for nonconformity he was confined to Bedford gaol. The local magistrates, anxious to establish

their identity as servants of the newly restored monarchy and about-to-be-restored Church of England, thought it good to make an example of Bedfordshire's most popular preacher, indicting and imprisoning him as a subversive who would not promise to preach at non-Anglican assemblies. In prison Bunyan had no heating and slept on straw, but he enjoyed fair health, kept cheerful, and wrote books. Also, to support his wife and children, he made 'many hundred grosse of long-tagged thread laces' which were then sold. Widely acknowledged as a man of spiritual authority, he counselled visitors, preached to the inmates regularly, and was sometimes let out to preach as well. Charles II's Declaration of Indulgence brought about his release in 1672. The church had formally appointed him pastor just before that, and pastoral ministry was his role for the rest of his life.

(3) The years 1672–88 were Bunyan's years of distinction, both as a preacher and as an author. *Pilgrim's Progress*, begun it seems during a further six month spell in prison in 1675, was published in 1678, and sold like hot cakes. *The Life and Death of Mr Badman* (1680), *The Holy War* (1682), and part two of *Pilgrim's Progress* (1684), confirmed Bunyan's standing as a writer not simply of devotional treatises in the well-known homiletic manner of a hundred Puritans before him, but of wonderfully vivid, racy, didactic-parabolic-allegorical stories which one way and another anchored evangelical faith in the world of common-man life. Altogether sixty books of different sorts came from Bunyan's pen during the thirty years of his writing career, and they are all worth reading still.

Something more must be said here about *Pilgrim's Progress*, which is both the best of Bunyan and a perfect pictorial index to the Puritan understanding of the Christian life. Secular study sees it as the start of the English novel, by reason of its quest-plot and its interplay of character, but Bunyan himself viewed it as a teaching tool — a didactic parable explaining the path of piety to ordinary people; a series of enlightening similitudes (Bunyan's word) about godliness and its opposite; a biblical dream tale with characters drawn from waking life to illustrate spiritual realities; a story that by God's grace might become the reader's own story as he or she went along. In the versified Apology that introduces part one, Bunyan tells us how it all started.

When at the first I took my Pen in hand
Thus for to write, I did not understand
That I at all should make a little Book
In such a mode; Nay, I had undertook
To make another, which when almost done
Before I was aware, I this begun.
And thus it was: I writing of the Way
and Race of Saints, in this our Gospel-Day,
Fell suddenly into an Allegory
About their Journey, and the way to Glory,
In more than twenty things, which I set down;
This done, I twenty more had in my Crown,
And they again began to multiply,
Like sparks that from the coals of fire do fly . . .
Thus I set Pen to Paper with delight,
And quickly had my thoughts in black and white,

For having now my Method by the end,
Still as I pull'd, it came; and so I penn'd
It down; until at last it came to be
For length and breadth the bigness which you see. . .
This Book it chalketh out before thine eyes
The man that seeks the everlasting Prize:
It shows you whence he comes, whither he goes,
What he leaves undone, also what he doth;
It also shows you how he runs and runs
Till he unto the Gate of Glory comes . . .
This book will make a Traveller of thee
If by its Counsel thou wilt ruled be;
It will direct thee to the Holy Land
If thou wilt its Directions understand . . .
Would'st read thyself, and read thou know'st not what
And yet know whether thou art blest or not
By reading the same lines? O then come hither
And lay my Book, thy Head, and Heart together.

'The man that seeks the everlasting Prize . . . runs and runs,' says Bunyan. Though the pilgrim in his story walks most of the way, he starts by running, once Evangelist has given him his first directions, and Bunyan makes a point of it: 'So I saw in my Dream, that the Man began to run . . . the Man put his fingers in his ears, and ran on crying, Life! Life! Eternal Life!' Running, for Bunyan, is a picture of wholehearted effort to get away from something dreadful and get to something wonderful; in that sense, the pilgrim runs constantly, even when the story shows him walking and talking, as most of the time it does. This brings us to *The Heavenly Footman*. 'Footman' here means, not flunkey or foot-soldier, but a traveller on foot ('Such footmen as thee and I are,' as Christian says to Hopeful); 'heavenly' means heading for heaven as the goal; and the piece itself is a written-up sermon on 1 Corinthians 9:24 of which the burden is, quite simply – run!

When Bunyan wrote it is not certain, for it was not published in his lifetime: his friend Charles Doe brought it out in 1692, four years after his death. But the thoughts that *The Footman* develops are so much an echo of *Pilgrim's Progress* that it is hard to doubt that the sermon was written very soon after Bunyan finished the allegory. George Offer, Bunyan's mid-nineteenth century editor, draws this out:

> Is there a Slough of Despond to be passed, and a hill Difficulty to be overcome? Here the footman is reminded of 'many a dirty step, many a high hill, a long and tedious journey through a vast howling wilderness;' but he is encouraged, 'the land of promise is at the end of the way.' Must the man that would win eternal glory draw his sword, put on his helmet, and fight his way into the temple – the heavenly footman must press, crowd, and thrust through all that stands between heaven and his soul. Did Ignorance, who perished from the way, say to the pilgrims, 'You go so fast, I must stay awhile behind?' He who runs to heaven is told that the heavy-heeled, lazy, wanton, and foolish professor will not attain the prize. The wicket-gate at the head of the way, is all-important; none can get to heaven unless they enter by Christ, the door and the way, so the footman is reminded that it matters not how fast he runs, he can never attain the prize, if he is

in the wrong road. Did the pilgrims so severely suffer from entering upon Byepath-meadow (*sic*), and even after that bitter experience were they again misled into a bye path, by a black man clothed in white raiment? Our footman is warned – Beware then of bye and crooked paths that lead to death and damnation . . . Did the poor pilgrims go grunting, puffing, and sighing, one tumbleth over a bush, another sticks fast in the dirt, one cries out, I am down, and another, Ho! where are you? So the footman is told that he will 'meet with cross, pain, and wearisomeness to the flesh, with briars and quagmires, and other encumbrances,' through all which he must persevere. Did Formalist and Hypocrite turn off into bye-ways at the foot of the hill Difficulty, and miserably perish? Did Mistrust and Timorous run back for fear of the persecuting lions, Church and State? So the man that runs for heaven is cautioned – 'Some when they come at the cross can go no further, but back again to their sins they go, stumble and break their necks, or turn aside to the left or to the right, and perish. Be not ready to halt, nor run hobbling . . .' Or, as Paul puts it in the text which this sermon opens up, 'So run, that ye may obtain.'

The Heavenly Footman, first to last, is a single sustained exhortation to run, to run hard, and to keep running, along the path of life. Bunyan assumes that his readers already know the objective truths of the gospel that *Pilgrim's Progress* pictures for them, and now concentrates on raising consciousness and generating commitment with regard to gaining heaven and escaping hell. Here, as in other of his homiletical writings, Bunyan's intensity almost overwhelms you. His sense of hell's horrors, and of the truth of God's threatenings to the careless and insincere that match his promises to the faithful, is tremendously strong, and he commands a flow of words that makes him more able than most to make us feel what he feels himself. It is truly 'awakening and converting work' that he is engaged in here. Having formulated the teaching of his text as *they that will have heaven must run for it*, he rings the changes of why and how to run, and deploys motivating thoughts that should set you and keep you running, and jolt you out of any complacent apathy, or laziness, or as he calls it slothfulness, that may have settled down on your spirit. Perhaps the most piercing of all his remarks about this are contained in 'An Epistle to All the Slothful and Careless People' which he prints as a foreword, but which he undoubtedly wrote after completing the book, while the thoughts he had deployed were still boiling in his mind. Feel the force of these extracts from it:

> This I dare to be bold to say, no greater shame can befall a man, than to see that he hath fooled away his soul, and sinned away eternal life. And I am sure this is the next (most direct) way to do it; namely, to be slothful; slothful, I say, in the work of salvation . . .

> If you would know a sluggard in the things of heaven, compare him with one that is slothful in the things of this world. As 1. He that is slothful is loth to set about the work he should follow: so is he that is slothful for heaven. 2. He that is slothful is one that is willing to make delays: so is he that is slothful for heaven. 3. He

that is a sluggard, any small matter that cometh in between, he will make it a sufficient excuse to keep him off from plying his work: so it is also with him that is slothful for heaven. 4. He that is slothful doth his work by the halves; and so it is in him that is slothful for heaven . . . 5. They that are slothful, do usually lose the season in which things are to be done: and thus it is also with them that are slothful for heaven, they miss the season of grace. And therefore, 6. They that are slothful have seldom or never good fruit, so also it will be with the soul-sluggard. 7. They that are slothful they are chid (rebuked) for the same: so also will Christ deal with those that are not active for him . . .

Arise man, be slothful no longer; set foot, and heart, and all into the way of God, and run, the crown is at the end of the race; there also standeth the loving forerunner, even Jesus, who hath prepared heavenly provision to make thy soul welcome, and he will give it thee with a more willing heart than ever thou canst desire it of him . . .

I wish our souls may meet with comfort at the journey's end.

This is the true, heartsearching, heartwarming John Bunyan, on full throttle, as indeed he is throughout this book. Let me not keep you from him, or him from you, any longer. As he says, heaven beckons: may we ever be found running for it.

J. I. Packer

THE HEAVENLY FOOTMAN

OR

A DESCRIPTION OF THE MAN
THAT GETS TO HEAVEN:
TOGETHER WITH
THE WAY HE RUNS IN, THE MARK HE
GOES BY;
ALSO
SOME DIRECTIONS HOW TO RUN SO
AS TO OBTAIN

JOHN BUNYAN

'And it came to pass, when they had brought them forth, that he said, Escape for thy life; look not behind thee, neither stay thou in all the plain: escape to the mountain lest thou be consumed'
Genesis 19:17

An epistle to all the slothful and careless people

Friends,

Solomon saith, that 'The desire of the slothful killeth him' (Proverbs 21:25); and if so, what will slothfulness itself do to those that entertain it? The proverb is, 'He that sleepeth in harvest is a son that causeth shame' (Proverbs 10:5). And this I dare be bold to say, no greater shame can befall a man than to see that he hath fooled away his soul and sinned away eternal life. And I am sure this is the next way to do it, namely, to be slothful; slothful, I say, in the work of salvation. The vineyard of the slothful man, in reference to the things of this life, is not fuller of briars, nettles and stinking weeds than he that is slothful for heaven hath his heart full of heart-choking and soul-damning sin.

Slothfulness hath these two evils: first, to neglect the time in which it should be getting of heaven; and by that means doth, in the second place, bring in untimely repentance. I will warrant you that he who shall lose his soul in this world through slothfulness will have no cause to be glad thereat when he comes to hell.

Slothfulness is usually accompanied with carelessness, and carelessness is for the most part begotten by senselessness; and senselessness doth again put fresh strength into slothfulness, and by this means the soul is left remediless.

Slothfulness shutteth out Christ; slothfulness shameth the soul (Canticles 5:2-4; Proverbs 13:4).

Slothfulness is condemned even by the feeblest of all the creatures: 'Go to the ant, thou sluggard, consider her ways and be wise' (Proverbs 6:6). 'The sluggard will not plough by reason of the cold' (Proverbs 20:4), that is, he will not break up the fallow ground of his heart because there must be some pains taken by him that will do it. 'Therefore shall he beg in harvest,' that is, when the saints of God shall have their glorious heaven and happiness given to them; but the sluggard shall 'have nothing', that is, be never the better for his crying for mercy, according to Matthew 25:10-12.

If you would know a sluggard in the things of heaven, compare him with one that is slothful in the things of this world. As,

1. He that is slothful is loathe to set about the work he should follow: so is he that is slothful for heaven.

2. He that is slothful is one that is willing to make delays: so is he that is slothful for heaven.

3. He that is a sluggard, any small matter that cometh in between, he will make it sufficient excuse to keep him off from plying his work: so is it also with him that is slothful for heaven.

4. He that is slothful doth his work by the halves: and so is it with him that is slothful for heaven. He may almost, but he shall never altogether, obtain perfection of deliverance from hell; he may almost, but he shall never, without he mend, be altogether a saint.

5. They that are slothful do usually lose the season in which things are to be done: and thus it is also with them that are slothful for heaven, they miss the season of grace. And therefore,

6. They that are slothful have seldom or never good fruit: so also it will be with the soul-sluggard.

7. They that are slothful they are chid for the same: so also will Christ deal with those that are not active for him. 'Thou wicked or slothful servant, out of thine own mouth will I judge thee; thou saidst I was thus, and thus, wherefore then gavest not thou my money to the bank?' (Luke 19:22). 'Take the unprofitable servant, and cast him into utter darkness, where shall be weeping and gnashing of teeth' (Matthew 25:26-30).

What shall I say? Time runs; and will you be slothful? Much of your lives are past; and will you be slothful? Your souls are worth a thousand worlds; and will you be slothful? The day of death and judgment is at the door; and will you be slothful? The curse of God hangs over your heads; and will you be slothful?

Besides, the devils are earnest, laborious, and seek by all means every day, by every sin, to keep you out of heaven, and hinder you of salvation; and will you be slothful? Also your neighbours are diligent for things that will perish; and will you be slothful for things that will endure for ever?

Would you be willing to be damned for slothfulness? Would you be willing that the angels of God should neglect to fetch your souls away to heaven when you lie a-dying, and the devils stand by ready to scramble for them? Was Christ slothful in the work of your redemption? Are his ministers slothful in tendering this unto you?

And, lastly, If all this will not move, I tell you God will not be slothful or negligent to damn you — 'whose damnation now of a long time slumbereth not' —nor will the devils neglect to fetch thee, nor hell neglect to shut its mouth upon thee.

Sluggard, art thou asleep still? Art thou resolved to sleep the sleep of death? Will neither tidings from heaven or hell awake thee? Wilt thou say still, 'Yet a little sleep, a little slumber,' and 'a little folding of the hands to sleep?' (Proverbs 6:10). Wilt thou yet turn thyself in thy sloth, as the door is turned upon the hinges? Oh that I was one that was skilful in lamentation, and had but a yearning heart towards thee, how would I pity thee! How would I bemoan thee; Oh that I could, with Jeremiah, let my eyes run down with rivers of water for thee! Poor soul, lost soul, dying soul, what a hard heart have I that I cannot mourn for thee! If thou shouldst lose but a limb, a child, or a friend, it would not be so much, but poor man it is *thy soul*: if it was to lie in hell but for a day, nay, ten thousand years, it would (in comparison) be nothing. But Oh it is for ever! Oh this cutting *ever*! What a soul-amazing word will that be, which saith, 'Depart from me, ye cursed, into *everlasting* fire'!

Objection. But if I should set in, and run as you would have me, then I must run from all my friends; for none of them are running that way.

Answer. And if thou dost, thou wilt run into the bosom of Christ and of God, and then what harm will that do thee?

Objection. But if I run this way, then I must run from all my sins.

Answer. That is true indeed; yet if thou dost not, thou wilt run into hell-fire.

Objection. But if I run this way, then I shall be hated, and lose the love of my friends and relations, and of those that I expect benefit from, or have reliance on, and I shall be mocked of all my neighbours.

Answer. And if thou dost not, thou art sure to lose the love and favour of God and Christ, the benefit of heaven and glory, and be mocked of God for thy folly; 'I also will laugh at your calamity; I will mock when your fear cometh;' and if thou wouldst not be hated and mocked, then take heed thou by thy folly dost not procure the displeasure and mocking of the great God; for his mocks and hatred will be terrible, because they will fall upon thee in terrible times, even when tribulation and anguish taketh hold on thee; which will be when death and judgment comes, when all the men in the earth, and all the angels in heaven, cannot help thee (Proverbs 1:26-28).

Objection. But surely I may begin this time enough, a year of two hence, may I not?

Answer. (1) Hast thou any lease of thy life? Did ever God tell thee thou shalt live half a year, or two months longer? Nay, it may be thou mayest not live so long.

And therefore, (2), Wilt thou be so sottish and unwise as to venture thy soul upon a little uncertain time?

(3) Dost thou know whether the day of grace will last a week longer or no? For the day of grace is past with some before their life is ended: and if it should be so with thee, wouldst thou not say, Oh that I had begun to run before the day of grace had been past and the gates of heaven shut against me.

But (4), If thou shouldst see any of thy neighbours neglect the making sure of either house or land to themselves, if they had it proffered to them, saying, 'Time enough hereafter,' when the time is uncertain; and besides, they do not know whether ever it will be proffered to them again, or no: I say, Wouldst thou not then call them fools? And if so, then dost thou think that thou art a wise man to let thy immortal soul hang over hell by a thread of uncertain time, which may soon be cut asunder by death?

But to speak plainly, all these are the words of a slothful spirit. Arise, man, be slothful no longer; set foot and heart and all into the way of God, and run, the crown is at the end of the race; there also standeth the loving forerunner, even Jesus, who hath prepared heavenly provision to make thy soul welcome, and he will give it thee with a more willing heart than ever thou can desire it of him. Oh therefore do not delay the time any longer, but put into practice the words of the men of Dan to their brethren, after they had seen the goodness of the land of Canaan: 'Arise,' say they, 'for we have seen the land, and behold it is very good; and are ye still.' Or do you forbear running? 'Be not slothful to go, and to enter to possess the land' (Judges 18:9). Farewell.

I wish our souls may meet with comfort at the journey's end.

John Bunyan

The Heavenly Footman

'So run that ye may obtain' (1 Corinthians 9:24).

Heaven and happiness is that which every one desireth, insomuch that wicked Balaam could say, 'Let me die the death of the righteous, and let my last end be like his' (Numbers 23:10). Yet for all this, there are but very few that do obtain that ever-to-be-desired glory, insomuch that many eminent professors drop short of a welcome from God into his pleasant place.

The apostle, therefore, because he did desire the salvation of the souls of the Corinthians, to whom he writes this epistle, layeth them down in these words, such counsel which, if taken, would be for their help and advantage. First, not to be wicked, and sit still, and wish for heaven; but *to run* for it. Second, not to content themselves with every kind of running; but saith he, '*So run*, that ye may obtain.' As if he should say, Some, because they would not lose their souls, begin to run betimes (Ecclesiastes 12:1); they run apace, they run with patience (Hebrews 12:1), they run the right way. Do you so run? Some run from both father and mother, friends and companions, and this, that they may have the crown. Do you so run? Some run through temptations, afflictions, good report, that they may win the pearl (1 Corinthians 4:13; 2 Corinthians 6). Do you so run? 'So run that ye may obtain.'

These words are taken from men's running for a wager: a very apt similitude to set before the eyes of the saints of the Lord. 'Know ye not that they which run in a race run all, but one receiveth the prize? So run, that ye may obtain.' That is, do not only run, but be sure you win as well as run. 'So run, that ye may obtain.'

I shall not need to make any great ado in opening the words at this time, but shall rather lay down one doctrine that I do find in them; and in prosecuting that, I shall show you, in some measure, the scope of the words.

1. The doctrine of the text

The doctrine is this: *they that will have heaven must run for it*; I say, they that will have heaven, they must run for it. I beseech you to heed it well. 'Know ye not that they which run in a race run all, but one receiveth the prize? So run ye.' The prize is heaven, and if you will have it, you must run for it. You have another scripture for this in Hebrews 12:1-3: 'Wherefore seeing we also,' saith the apostle, 'are compassed about with so great a cloud of witnesses, let us lay aside every weight, and the sin which doth so easily beset us, and let us run with patience the race that is set before us.' And *let us run*, saith he. Again, saith Paul, 'I therefore so run, not as uncertainly, so fight I...'

2. The word *run* opened

But before I go any further, observe:

First — *flying*: that this running is not an ordinary or any sort of running, but it is to be understood of the swiftest sort of running; and therefore in Hebrews 6 it is called 'a fleeing': that 'we might have a strong consolation, who have fled for refuge, to lay hold upon the hope set before us.' Mark, 'who have fled.' It is taken from that Joshua 20, concerning the man that was to flee to the city of refuge when the avenger of blood was hard at his heels to take vengeance on him for the offence he had committed; therefore it is a *running* or *flying* for one's life. A running with all might and main, as we use to say. So run!

Second — *pressing*: This running in another place is called a pressing: 'I press toward the mark' (Philippians 3:14), which signifieth that they that will have heaven must not stick at any difficulties they meet with; but press, crowd, and thrust through all that may stand between heaven and their souls. So run!

Third — *continuing*. This running is called in another place 'a continuing in the way of life. If ye continue in the faith grounded, and settled, and be not moved away from the hope of the gospel' of Christ (Colossians 1:23). Not to run a little now and then, by fits and starts, or halfway, or almost thither; but to run for my life, to run through all difficulties, and to continue therein to the end of the race, which must be to the end of my life. 'So run, that ye may obtain.'

3. Several reasons for clearing this doctrine

And the reasons for this point are these:

First, because all or every one that runneth doth not obtain the prize; there be many that do run, yea, and run far too, who yet miss of the crown that standeth at the end of the race. You know that all that run in a race do not obtain the victory; they all run, but one wins. And so it is here; it is not everyone that runneth, nor every one that seeketh, nor every one that striveth for the mastery that hath it. (Luke 13). Though a man do strive for the mastery, saith Paul, 'yet he is not crowned, except he strive lawfully;' that is, unless he so run, and so strive, as to have God's approbation (2 Timothy 2:5). What, do you think that every heavy-heeled professor will have heaven? What, every lazy one, every wanton and foolish professor, that will be stopped by anything, kept back by anything, that scarce runneth so fast heavenward as a snail creepeth on the ground? Nay, there are some professors do not go on so fast in the way of God as a snail doth go on the wall; and yet these think that heaven and happiness is for them. But stay, there are many more that run than there be that obtain; therefore, he that will have heaven must *run* for it.

Second, because you know that though a man do run, yet if he do not overcome, or win, as well as run, what will he be the better for his running? He will get nothing. You know the man that runneth, he doth do it that he may win the prize; but if he doth not obtain, he doth lose his labour, spend his pains and time and that to no purpose; I say, he getteth nothing. And ah! how many such runners will there be found at the day of judgment! Even multitudes, multitudes that have run, yea, run as far as to come to heaven's gates, and not able to get any further, but there stand knocking, when it is too late, crying, Lord, Lord, when they will have nothing but rebukes for their pains. Depart from me, you come not here, you come too late, you run too lazily; the door is shut. 'When once the master of the house is risen up,' saith Christ, 'and hath shut to the door, and ye begin to stand without, and to knock at the door, saying, "Lord, Lord, open unto us," I will say, "I know ye not, Depart…"' (Luke 13:25). Oh sad will the estate of those be that run and miss; therefore, if you will have heaven, you must run for it; and 'so run that ye may obtain.'

Third, because the way is long (I speak metaphorically), and there is many a dirty step, many a high hill, much work to do, a wicked heart, world, and devil, to overcome; I say there are many steps to be taken by those that intend to be saved, by running or walking, in the steps of that faith of our father Abraham. Out of Egypt thou must go through the Red Sea; thou must run a long and tedious journey through the vast howling wilderness before thou come to the land of promise.

Fourth, they that will go to heaven they must run for it; because, as the way is long, so the time in which they are to get to the end of it is very uncertain; the time present is the only time; thou hast no more time allotted thee than that thou now enjoyest. 'Boast not thyself of tomorrow, for thou knowest not what a day may bring forth' (Proverbs 27:1). Do not say, I have time enough to get to heaven seven years hence; for I tell thee the bell may toll for thee before seven days more be ended; and when death comes, away thou must go, whether thou art provided or not; and therefore look to it; make no delays; it is not good dallying with things of so great concernment as the salvation or damnation of thy soul. You know he that hath a great way to go in a little time, and less by half than he thinks of, he had need *run* for it.

Fifth, they that will have heaven must run for it because the devil, the law, sin, death and hell follow them. There is never a poor soul that is going to heaven, but the devil, the law, sin, death and hell, make after that soul. 'Your adversary, the devil, as a roaring lion, walketh about, seeking whom he may devour' (1 Peter 5:8). And I will assure you, the devil is nimble, he can run apace, he is light of foot, he hath overtaken many, he hath turned up their heels, and hath given them an everlasting fall. Also the law, that can shoot a great way, have a care thou keep out of the reach of those great guns, the ten commandments. Hell also hath a wide mouth; it can stretch itself further than you are aware of. And as the angel said to Lot, Take heed, 'Look not behind thee, neither tarry thou in all the plain,' that is, anywhere between this and heaven, 'lest thou be consumed' (Genesis 19:17). So say I to thee, Take heed, tarry not, lest either the devil, hell, death or the fearful curses of the law of God do overtake thee and throw thee down in the midst of thy sins so as never to rise and recover again. If this were well considered, then thou, as well as I, wouldst say, they that will have heaven must run for it.

Sixth, they that will go to heaven must run for it because perchance the gates of heaven may be shut shortly. Sometimes sinners have not heaven's gates open to them so long as they suppose; and if they be once shut against a man, they are so heavy that all the men in the world, nor all the angels in heaven, are not able to open them. I shut, 'and no man openeth,' saith Christ. And how if thou shouldst come but one quarter of an hour too late? I tell thee, it will cost thee an eternity to bewail thy misery in. Francis Spira can tell thee what it is to stay till the gate of mercy be quite shut; or to run so lazily, that they be shut before thou get within them. What, to be shut out! What, out of heaven! Sinner, rather than lose it, run for it; yea, and 'so run that thou mayest obtain.'

Seventh, because if thou lose, thou losest all; thou losest soul, God, Christ, heaven, ease, peace. Besides, thou layest thyself open to all the shame, contempt and reproach that either God, Christ, saints, the world, sin, the devil and all can lay upon thee. As Christ saith of the foolish builder, so will I say of thee, if thou be such a one who runs and misses; I say, even all that go by will begin to mock at thee, saying, This man began to run well, but was not able to finish (Luke 14:28-30). But more of this anon.

Question. But how should a poor soul do to run? For this very thing is that which afflicteth me sore, as you say, to think that I may run and yet fall short. Methinks to fall short at last, Oh, it fears me greatly. Pray tell me, therefore, how I should run.

Answer. That thou mightest indeed be satisfied in this particular, consider these following things.

4. Nine directions how to run

The First Direction

If thou wouldst so run as to obtain the kingdom of heaven, then be sure that thou get into the way that leadeth thither. For it is a vain thing to think that ever thou shalt have the prize, though thou runnest never so fast, unless thou art in the way that leads to it. Set the case, that there should be a man in London that was to run to York for a wager; now, though he run never so swiftly, yet if he run full south, he might run himself quickly out of breath, and be never the nearer the prize, but rather the further off. Just so is it here; it is not simply the runner, nor yet the hasty runner, that winneth the crown, unless he be in the way that leadeth thereto. I have observed, that little time which I have been a professor, that there is a great running to and fro, some this way, and some that way, yet it is to be feared most of them are out of the way, and then, though they run as swift as the eagle can fly, they are benefited nothing at all.

Here is one runs a-quaking, another a-ranting; one again runs after the Baptism, and another after the Independency. Here is one for free will, and another for Presbytery; and yet possibly most of all these sects run quite the wrong way, and yet every one is for his life, his soul, either for heaven or hell.

If thou now say, Which is the way? I tell thee it is CHRIST, THE SON OF MARY, THE SON OF GOD. Jesus saith, 'I am the way, and the truth, and the life; no man cometh unto the Father but by me' (John 14:6). So then thy business, is if thou wouldst hear salvation, to see if Christ be thine, with all his benefits; whether he hath covered thee with his righteousness, whether he hath showed thee that thy sins are washed away with his heart-blood, whether thou art planted into him, and whether thou have faith in him, so as to make a life out of him, and to conform thee to him. That is, such faith as to conclude that thou art righteous, because Christ is thy righteousness, and so constrained to walk with him as the joy of thy heart, because he saveth thy soul. And for the Lord's sake take heed, and do not deceive thyself, and think thou art in the way upon too slight grounds; for if thou miss of the way, thou wilt miss of the prize; and if thou miss of that, I am sure thou wilt lose thy soul, even that soul which is worth more than the whole world.

But I have treated more largely on this in my book of the two covenants, and therefore shall pass it now; only I beseech thee to have a care of thy soul, and that thou mayest so do, take this counsel: Mistrust thy own strength, and throw it away; down on thy knees in prayer to the Lord for the spirit of truth; search his word for direction; fly seducer's company; keep company with the soundest Christians, that have most experience of Christ; and be sure thou have a care of Quakers, Ranters, Freewillers;

also do not have too much company with some Anabaptists, though I go under that name myself. I tell thee this is such a serious matter, and I fear thou wilt so little regard it, that the thoughts of the worth of the thing, and of thy too light regarding of it, doth even make my heart ache whilst I am writing to thee. The Lord teach thee the way by his Spirit, and then I am sure thou wilt know it. *So run.*

Only by the way, let me bid thee have a care of two things, and so I shall pass to the next thing.

1. Have a care of relying on the outward obedience to any of God's commands, or thinking thyself ever the better in the sight of God for that.

2. Take heed of fetching peace for thy soul from any inherent righteousness; but if thou can believe that as thou art a sinner, so thou art justified freely by the love of God, through the redemption that is in Christ; and that God for Christ's sake hath forgiven thee, not because he saw any thing done, or to be done, in or by thee, to move him thereunto to do it; for that is the right way; the Lord put thee into it, and keep thee in it.

The Second Direction

As thou shouldst get into the way so thou shouldst also be much in studying and musing on the way. You know men that would be expert in any thing, they are usually much in studying of that thing, and so likewise is it with those that quickly grow expert in any way. This therefore thou shouldst do; let thy study be much exercised about Christ, which is the way; what he is, what he hath done, and why he is what he is, and why he hath done what is done; as, why 'He took upon him the form of a servant,' why he 'was made in the likeness of men' (Philippians 2:7)? Why he cried; why he died; why he bore the sin of the world; why he was made sin, and why he was made righteousness; why he is in heaven in the nature of man, and what he doth there (2 Corinthians 5:21)?

Be much in musing and considering of these things; be thinking also enough of those places which thou must not come near, but leave some on this hand, and some on that hand; as it is with those that travel into other countries, they must leave such a gate on this hand, and such a bush on that hand, and go by such a place, where standeth such a thing. Thus, therefore, thou must do: Avoid such things which are expressly forbidden in the Word of God. 'Withdraw thy foot far from her, and come not nigh the door of her house, for her steps take hold on hell, going down to the chambers of death' (Proverbs 5:7). And so of every thing that is not in the way, have a care of it, that thou go not by it; come not near it, have nothing to do with it. *So run.*

The Third Direction

Not only thus, but, in the next place, thou must strip thyself of those things that may hang upon thee to the hindering of thee in the way to the kingdom of heaven, as covetousness, pride, lust, or whatever else thy heart may be inclining unto, which may hinder thee in this heavenly race. Men that run for a wager, if they intend to win as well as run, they do not use to encumber themselves, or carry those things about them that may be a hindrance to them in their running. 'Every man that striveth for the mastery is temperate in all things' (1 Corinthians 9:25), that is, he layeth aside every thing that would be any ways a disadvantage to him; as saith the apostle, 'Let us lay aside every weight, and the sin which doth so easily beset us, and let us run with patience the race that is set before us' (Hebrews 12:1).

It is but a vain thing to talk of going to heaven, if thou let thy heart be encumbered with those things that would hinder. Would you not say that such a man would be in danger of losing, though he run, if he fill his pockets with stones, hang heavy garments on his shoulders, and great lumpish shoes on his feet? So is it here, thou talkest of going to heaven, and yet fillest thy pockets with stones, i.e., fillest thy heart with this world, lettest that hang on thy shoulders, with its profits and pleasures. Alas, alas, thou art widely mistaken! If thou intendest to win, thou must strip, thou must lay aside every weight, thou must be temperate in all things. Thou must *so run*.

The Fourth Direction

Beware of by-paths; take heed thou dost not turn into those lanes which lead out of the way. There are crooked paths, paths in which men go astray, paths that lead to death and damnation, but take heed of all those (Isaiah 59:8). Some of them are dangerous because of practice (Proverbs 7:25); some because of opinion, but mind them not; mind the path before thee, look right before thee, turn neither to the right hand nor to the left, but let thine eyes look right on, even right before thee (Proverbs 3:17). 'Ponder the path of thy feet, and let all thy ways be established. Turn not to the right hand nor to the left. Remove thy foot far from evil' (Proverbs 4:26, 27).

This counsel being not so seriously taken as given, is the reason of that starting from opinion to opinion, reeling this way and that way, out of this lane into that lane, and so missing the way to the kingdom. Though the way to heaven be but one, yet there are many crooked lanes and by-paths shoot down upon it, as I may say. And again, notwithstanding the kingdom of heaven be the biggest city, yet usually those by-paths are most beaten, most travellers go those ways; and therefore the way to heaven is hard to be found, and as hard to be kept in, by reason of these. Yet, nevertheless, it is in this case as it was with the harlot of Jericho; she had one scarlet thread tied in her window, by which her house was known (Joshua 2:18).

So it is here, the scarlet streams of Christ's blood run throughout the way to the kingdom of heaven; therefore mind that, see if thou do find the besprinkling of the blood of Christ in the way, and if thou do, be of good cheer, thou art in the right way; but have a care thou beguile not thyself with a fancy, for then thou mayest light into any lane or way; but that thou mayest not be mistaken, consider, though it seem never so pleasant, yet if thou do not find that in the very middle of the road there is writing with the heart-blood of Christ, that he came into the world to save sinners, and that we are justified, though we are ungodly; shun that way; for this it is which the apostle meaneth when he saith, We have 'boldness to enter into the holiest by the blood of Jesus, by a new and living way which he hath consecrated for us, through the veil, that is to say, his flesh' (Hebrews 10:19,20).

How easy a matter is it in this our day, for the devil to be too cunning for poor souls, by calling his by-paths the way to the kingdom! If such an opinion or fancy be but cried up by one or more, this inscription being set upon it by the devil, 'This is the way of God,' how speedily, greedily, and by heaps, do poor simple souls throw away themselves upon it; especially if it be daubed over with a few external acts of morality, if so good. But this is because men do not know painted by-paths from the plain way to the kingdom of heaven. They have not yet learned the true Christ, and what his righteousness is, neither have they a sense of their own insufficiency; but are bold, proud, presumptuous, self-conceited. And therefore,

The Fifth Direction

Do not thou be too much in looking too high in thy journey heavenwards. You know men that run in a race do not use to stare and gaze this way and that, neither do they use to cast up their eyes too high, lest happily, through their too much gazing with their eyes after other things, they in the meantime stumble and catch a fall. The very same case is this; if thou gaze and stare after every opinion and way that comes into the world; also if thou be prying overmuch into God's secret decrees, or let thy heart too much entertain questions about some nice foolish curiosities, thou mayest stumble and fall, as many hundreds in England have done, both in Ranting and Quakery, to their own eternal overthrow; without the marvellous operation of

God's grace be suddenly stretched forth to bring them back again.

Take heed therefore; follow not that proud and lofty spirit, that, devil-like, cannot be content with his own station. David was of an excellent spirit where he saith, 'Lord, my heart is not haughty, nor mine eyes lofty, neither do I exercise myself in great matters, or in things too high for me. Surely I have behaved and quieted myself as a child that is weaned of his mother: my soul is even as a weaned child' (Psalm 131:1,2). Do thou *so run*.

The Sixth Direction

Take heed that you have not an ear open to every one that calleth after you as you are in your journey. Men that run, you know, if any do call after them, saying, I would speak with you, or go not too fast, and you shall have my company with you, if they run for some great matter, they use to say, Alas, I cannot stay, I am in haste, pray talk not to me now; neither can I stay for you, I am running for a wager: if I win I am made, if I lose I am undone, and therefore hinder me not. Thus wise are men when they run for corruptible things, and thus should thou do, and thou hast more cause to do so than they, forasmuch as they run but for things that last not, but thou for an incorruptible glory.

I give thee notice of this betimes, knowing that thou shalt have enough call after thee, even the devil, sin, this world, vain company, pleasures, profits, esteem among men, ease, pomp, pride, together with an innumerable company of such companions; one crying, Stay for me;

the other saying, Do not leave me behind; a third saying, And take me along with you. What, will you go, saith the devil, without your sins, pleasures, and profits? Are you so hasty? Can you not stay and take these along with you? Will you leave your friends and companions behind you? Can you not do as your neighbours do, carry the world, sin, lust, pleasure, profit, esteem among men, along with you? Have a care thou do not let thine ear now be open to the tempting, enticing, alluring, and soul-entangling flatteries of such sink-souls as these are. 'My son,' saith Solomon, 'if sinners entice thee, consent thou not' (Proverbs 1:10).

You know what it cost the young man which Solomon speaks of in the 7th of the Proverbs, that was enticed by a harlot, 'With her much fair speech she' won him, and 'caused him to yield, with the flattering of her lips she forced him,' till he went after her 'as an ox to the slaughter, or as a fool to the correction of the stocks;' even so far, 'till the dart struck through his liver, and knew not that it was for his life. Hearken unto me now therefore,' saith he, 'Oh ye children, and attend to the words of my mouth, let not thine heart decline to her ways, go not astray in her paths, for she hath cast down many wounded, yea, many strong men have been slain by her,' that is, kept out of heaven by her, 'her house is the way to hell, going down to the chambers of death.'

Soul, take this counsel and say, Satan, sin, lust, pleasure, profit, pride, friends, companions, and everything else, let me alone, stand off, come not nigh me, for I am running for heaven, for my soul, for God, for Christ, from hell, and everlasting damnation: if I win, I win all, and if I lose, I lose all; let me alone, for I will not hear. *So run.*

The Seventh Direction

In the next place, be not daunted though thou meetest with never so many discouragements in thy journey thither. That man that is resolved for heaven, if Satan cannot win him by flatteries, he will endeavour to weaken him by discouragements; saying, thou art a sinner, thou hast broke God's law, thou art not elected, thou comest too late, the day of grace is past, God doth not care for thee, thy heart is naught, thou art lazy, with a hundred other discouraging suggestions.

And thus it was with David, where he saith, 'I had fainted, unless I had believed to see the goodness of the Lord in the land of the living' (Psalm 27:13,14). As if he should say, the devil did so rage and my heart was so base, that had I judged according to my own sense and feeling, I had been absolutely distracted; but I trusted to Christ in the promise, and looked that God would be as good as his promise, in having mercy upon me, an unworthy sinner; and this is that which encouraged me, and kept me from fainting.

And thus must thou do when Satan, or the law, or thy own conscience, do go about to dishearten thee, either by the greatness of thy sins, the wickedness of thy heart, the tediousness of the way, the loss of outward enjoyments, the hatred that thou wilt procure from the world, or the like; then thou must encourage thyself with the freeness of the promises, the tender-heartedness of Christ, the merits of his blood, the freeness of his invitations to come in, the greatness of the sin of others that have been pardoned, and that the same God, through the same Christ, holdeth forth the same grace free as ever. If these be not thy meditations, thou wilt draw very heavily in the way to heaven if thou do not give up all for lost, and so knock off from following any farther; therefore, I say, take heart in thy journey, and say to them that seek thy destruction, 'Rejoice not against me, Oh mine enemy, when I fall I shall arise, when I sit in darkness the Lord shall be a light unto me' (Micah 7:8). *So run.*

The Eighth Direction

Take heed of being offended at the cross that thou must go by, before thou come to heaven. You must understand, as I have already touched, that there is no man that goeth to heaven but he must go by the cross. The cross is the standing way-mark by which all they that go to glory must pass by. 'We must through much tribulation enter into the kingdom of God' (Acts 14:22). 'Yea, and all that will live godly in Christ Jesus shall suffer persecution' (2 Timothy 3:12). If thou art in the way to the kingdom, my life for thine thou wilt come at the cross shortly – the Lord grant thou dost not shrink at it, so as to turn thee back again. 'If any man will come after me,' saith Christ, 'let him deny himself, and take up his cross daily, and follow me' (Luke 9:23).

The cross it stands, and hath stood, from the beginning, as a way-mark to the kingdom of heaven. You know if one ask you the way to such and such a place, you, for the better direction, do not only say, this is the way, but then also say, you must go by such a gate, by such a style, such a bush, tree, bridge, or such like. Why, so it is here; art thou inquiring the way to heaven? Why, I tell thee, Christ is the way; into him thou must get, into his righteousness, to be justified; and if thou art in him, thou wilt presently see the cross, thou must go close by it, thou must touch it, nay, thou must take it up, or else thou quickly go out of the way that leads to heaven, and turn up some of those crooked lanes that lead down to the chambers of death.

How thou mayest know the cross by these six things.

1. It is known in the doctrine of justification.
2. In the doctrine of mortification.
3. In the doctrine of perseverance.
4. In self-denial.
5. Patience.
6. Communion with poor saints.

1. *In the doctrine of justification*; there is a great deal of the cross in that: a man is forced to suffer the destruction of his own righteousness for the righteousness of another. This is no easy matter for a man to do; I assure to you it stretcheth every vein in his heart before he will be brought to yield to it. What, for a man to deny, reject, abhor, and throw away all his prayers, tears, alms, keeping of sabbaths, hearing, reading, with the rest, in the point of justification, and to count them accursed; and to be willing, in the very midst of the sense of his sins, to throw himself wholly upon the righteousness and obedience of another man,

abhorring his own, counting it as deadly sin, as the open breach of the law; as I say, to do this, in deed and in truth, is the biggest piece of the cross; and therefore Paul calleth this very thing a suffering; where he saith, 'And I have *suffered* the loss of all things,' which principally was his righteousness, 'that I might win Christ, and be found in him, not having,' but rejecting, 'mine own righteousness' (Philippians 3:8,9). That is the first.

2. *In the doctrine of mortification* is also much of the cross. Is it nothing for a man to lay hands on his vile opinions, on his vile sins, of his bosom sins, of his beloved, pleasant, darling sins, that stick as close to him, as the flesh sticketh to the bones? What, to lose all these brave things that my eyes behold, for that which I never saw with my eyes? What, to lose my pride, my covetousness, my vain company, sports, and pleasures, and the rest? I tell you this is no easy matter; if it were, what need all those prayers, sighs, watchings? What need we be so backward to it? Nay, do you not see, that some men, before they will set about this work, they will even venture the loss of their souls, heaven, God, Christ, and all? What means else all those delays and put-offs saying, Stay a little longer, I am loth to leave my sins while I am so young, and in health? Again, what is the reason else, that others do it so by the halves, coldly and seldom, notwithstanding they are convinced over and over; nay, and also promise to amend, and yet all's in vain? I will assure you, to cut off right hands, and to pluck out right eyes, is no pleasure to the flesh.

3. *The doctrine of perseverance* is also cross to the flesh; which is not only to begin, but for to hold out, not only

to bid fair, and to say, Would I had heaven, but so to know Christ, to put on Christ, and walk with Christ as to come to heaven. Indeed, it is no great matter to begin to look for heaven, to begin to seek the Lord, to begin to shun sin. Oh but it is a very great matter to continue with God's approbation! 'My servant Caleb,' saith God, is a man of 'another spirit, he hath followed me,' followed me always, he hath continually followed me, 'fully, he shall possess the land' (Numbers 14:24). Almost all the many thousands of the children of Israel in their generation, fell short of perseverance when they walked from Egypt towards the land of Canaan. Indeed they went to the work at first pretty willingly, they were quickly out of breath, and in their hearts they turned back again into Egypt.

It is an easy matter for a man to run hard for a spurt, for a furlong, for a mile or two; Oh, but to hold out for a hundred, for a thousand, for ten thousand miles; that man that doth this, he must look to meet with cross, pain, and wearisomeness to the flesh, especially if as he goeth he meeteth with briars and quagmires, and other incumbrances, that make his journey so much the more painful.

Nay, do you not see with your eyes daily, that perseverance is a very great part of the cross? Why else do men so soon grow weary? I could point out a many, that after they have followed the ways of God about a twelvemonth, others it may be two, three, or four, some more, and some less years, they have been beat out of wind, have taken up their lodging and rest before they have got halfway to heaven, some in this, and some in that sin;

and have secretly, nay sometimes openly said, that the way is too strait, the race too long, the religion too holy, and cannot hold out, I can go no farther.

4,5,6. And so likewise of the other three, to wit, patience, self-denial, communion, and communication with and to the poor saints. How hard are these things? It is an easy matter to deny another man, but it is not so easy a matter to deny one's self; to deny myself out of love to God, to his gospel, to his saints, of this advantage, and of that gain; nay, of that which otherwise I might lawfully do, were it not for offending them. That scripture is but seldom read, and seldomer put into practice, which saith, 'I will eat no flesh while the world standeth, if it make my brother to offend' (1 Corinthians 8:13). Again, 'We that are strong ought to bear the infirmities of the weak, and not to please ourselves' (Romans 15:1). But how froward, how hasty, how peevish, and self-resolved are the generality of professors at this day!

Also, how little considering the poor, unless it be to say, Be thou warmed and filled! But to give is a seldom work; also especially to give to any poor (Galatians 6:10). I tell you all things are cross to flesh and blood; and that man that hath but a watchful eye over the flesh, and also some considerable measure of strength against it, he shall find his heart in these things like unto a starting horse, that is rid without a curbing bridle, ready to start at everything that is offensive to him; yea, and ready to run away too, do what the rider can.

It is the cross which keepeth those that are kept from heaven. I am persuaded, were it not for the cross, where we have one professor, we should have twenty; but this cross, that is it which spoileth all.

Some men, as I said before, when they come at the cross they can go no farther, but back again to their sins they must go. Others they stumble at it, and break their necks; others again, when they see the cross is approaching, they turn aside to the left hand, or to the right hand, and so think to get to heaven another way; but they will be deceived. 'Yea, and all that will live godly in Christ Jesus *shall*,' mark, shall be sure to 'suffer persecution' (2 Timothy 3:12).

There are but few when they come at the cross, cry, 'Welcome, cross,' as some of the martyrs did to the stake they were burned at. Therefore, if thou meet with the cross in thy journey, in what manner soever it be, be not daunted, and say, Alas, what shall I do now! But rather take courage, knowing that by the cross is the way to the kingdom. Can a man believe in Christ and not be hated by the devil? Can he make a profession of this Christ, and that sweetly and convincingly, and the children of Satan hold their tongue? Can darkness agree with light? or the devil endure that Christ Jesus should be honoured both by faith and a heavenly conversation, and let that soul alone at quiet? Did you never read, that 'the dragon persecuteth the woman?' (Revelation 12). And that Christ saith, 'In the world ye shall have tribulation' (John 16:33).

The Ninth Direction

Beg of God that he would do these two things for thee: First, Enlighten thine understanding. And, Second, Inflame thy will. If these two be but effectually done, there is no fear but thou will go safe to heaven.

1. Enlighten thine understanding. One of the great reasons why men and women do so little regard the other world, it is because they see so little of it. And the reason why they see so little of it is because they have their understandings darkened. And therefore, saith Paul, do not you believers 'walk as do other Gentiles, even in the vanity of their minds, having the understanding darkened, being alienated from the life of God through the ignorance,' or foolishness 'that is in them, because of the blindness of their heart' (Ephesians 4:17,18). Walk not as those, run not with them: also, poor souls, they have their understandings darkened, their hearts blinded, and that is the reason they have such undervaluing thoughts of the Lord Jesus Christ, and the salvation of their souls.

For when men do come to see the things of another world, what a God, what a Christ, what a heaven, and what an eternal glory there is to be enjoyed; also when they see that it is possible for them to have a share in it, I tell you it will make them run through thick and thin to enjoy it. Moses, having a sight of this, because his understanding was enlightened, he feared not the wrath of the king, but chose 'rather to suffer affliction with the people of God, than to enjoy the pleasures of sin for a season'. He refused to be called the son of the king's daughter; accounting it wonderful riches to be counted worthy of so much as to suffer for Christ, with the poor despised saints; and that was because he saw him who was invisible, and 'had respect unto the recompense of the reward' (Hebrews 11:24-27).

And this is that which the apostle usually prayeth for in his epistles for the saints, namely, 'That they might know what is the hope of God's calling, and the riches of the glory of his inheritance in the saints' (Ephesians 3:18,19). Pray therefore that God would enlighten thy understanding: that will be very great help unto thee. It will make thee endure many a hard brunt for Christ; as Paul saith, 'After ye were illuminated, ye endured a great fight of afflictions. You took joyfully the spoiling of your goods, knowing in yourselves that ye have in heaven a better and an enduring substance' (Hebrews 10:32-34).

If there be never such a rare jewel lie just in a man's way, yet if he sees it not, he will rather trample upon it than stoop for it, and it is because he sees it not. Why, so it is here, though heaven be worth never so much, and thou hast never so much need of it, yet if thou see it not, that is, have not thy understanding opened or enlightened to see it, thou wilt not regard at all; therefore cry to the Lord for enlightening grace, and say, Lord, open my blind eyes: Lord, take the veil off my dark heart, show me the things of the other world, and let me see the sweetness, glory, and excellency of them for Christ his sake. This is the first.

2. *Inflame thy will*. Cry to God that he would inflame thy will also with the things of the other world. For when a man's will is fully set to do such or such a thing, then it must be a very hard matter that shall hinder that man from bringing about his end. When Paul's will was set resolvedly to go up to Jerusalem, though it was signified to him before what he should there suffer, he was not daunted at all; nay, saith he, 'I am ready,' or willing, 'not to be bound only,

but also to die at Jerusalem for the name of the Lord Jesus' (Acts 21:13). His will was inflamed with love to Christ; and therefore all the persuasions that could be used wrought nothing at all.

Your self-willed people nobody knows what to do with them; we used to say, He will have his own will, do all what you can. Indeed to have such a will for heaven, is an admirable advantage to a man that undertakes the race thither; a man that is resolved, and hath his will fixed, saith he, I will do my best to advantage myself; I will do my worst to hinder my enemies; I will not give out as long as I can stand; I will have it or I will lose my life; 'though he slay me, yet will I trust in him' (Job 13:15). 'I will not let thee go except thou bless me' (Genesis 32:26). *I will, I will, I will*, Oh this blessed inflamed will for heaven! What is like it? If a man be willing, then any argument shall be matter of encouragement; but if unwilling, then any argument shall give discouragement; this is seen both in saints and sinners; in them that are the children of God, and also those that are the children of the devil. As,

(1) The saints of old, they being willing, and resolved for heaven, what could stop them? Could fire or faggot, sword or halter, stinking dungeons, whips, bears, bulls, lions, cruel rackings, stoning, starving, nakedness (Hebrews 11). 'Nay, in all these things they were more than conquerors, through him that loved them' (Romans 8:37), who had also made them 'willing in the day of his power'.

(2) See again, on the other side, the children of the devil, because they are not willing (to run to heaven), how

many shifts and starting-holes they will have. I have married a wife, I have a farm, I shall offend my landlord, I shall offend my master, I shall lose my trading, I shall lose my pride, my pleasures, I shall be mocked and scoffed, therefore I dare not come. I, saith another, will stay till I am older, till my children are out of sight, till I am got a little aforehand in the world, till I have done this and that, and the other business; but alas, the thing is, they are not willing; for were they but soundly willing, these, and a thousand such as these, would hold them no faster than the cords held Samson when he broke them like burned flax (Judges 15:14).

I tell you the will is all; that is one of the chief things which turns the wheel either backwards or forwards; and God knoweth that full well, and so likewise doth the devil; and therefore they both endeavour very much to strengthen the will of their servants. God, he is for making of his a willing people to serve him; and the devil, he doth what he can to possess the will and affection of those that are his, with love to sin; and therefore when Christ comes close to the matter, indeed, saith he, 'Ye will not come to me' (John 5:40). 'How often would I have gathered you as a hen *doth* her chickens, and ye would not' (Luke 13:34). The devil had possessed their wills, and so long he was sure enough of them.

Oh therefore cry hard to God to inflame thy will for heaven and Christ: thy will, I say, if that be rightly set for heaven, you wilt not be beat off with discouragements; and this was the reason that, when Jacob wrestled with the angel, though he lost a limb, as it were, and the hollow of his thigh was put out of joint, as he wrestled with him, yet, saith he, 'I will not,' mark, 'I *will not* let thee go except thou bless me' (Genesis 32:24-26). Get thy will tipt with the heavenly grace, and resolution against all discouragements, and then thou goest full speed for heaven; but if thou falter in thy will, and be not found there, thou wilt run hobbling and halting all the way thou runnest, and also to be sure thou wilt fall short at the last. The Lord give thee a will and courage!

Thus have I done with directing thee how to run to the kingdom; be sure thou keep in memory what I have said unto thee, lest thou lose thy way. But because I would have thee think of them, take all in short in this little bit of paper.

1. Get into the way.

2. Then study on it.

3. Then strip, and lay aside everything that would hinder.

4. Beware of by-paths.

5. Do not gaze and stare too much about thee, and be sure to ponder the path of thy feet.

6. Do not stop for any that call after thee, whether it be the world, the flesh, or the devil; for all these will hinder thy journey, if possible.

7. Be not daunted with any discouragements thou meetest with as thou goest.

8. Take heed of stumbling at the cross.

9. Cry hard to God for an enlightened heart, and a willing mind, and God give thee a prosperous journey. Yet before I do quite take leave of thee, let me give thee a few motives along with thee. It may be they will be as good as a pair of spurs to prick on thy lumpish heart in this rich voyage.

5. Nine motives to urge us on in the way

The First Motive

Consider there is no way but this, thou must either win or lose. If thou winnest, then heaven, God, Christ, glory, ease, peace, life, yea, life eternal, is thine; thou must be made equal to the angel in heaven; thou shalt sorrow no more, sigh no more, feel no more pain; thou shalt be out of reach of sin, hell, death, the devil, the grave, and whatever else may endeavour thy hurt. But contrariwise, and if thou lose, then thy loss is heaven, glory, God, Christ, ease, peace, and whatever else which tendeth to make eternity comfortable to the saints; besides thou procurest eternal death, sorrow, pain, blackness, and darkness, fellowship with devils, together with the everlasting damnation of thy soul.

The Second Motive

Consider that this devil, this hell, death and damnation, followeth after thee as hard as they can drive, and have their commission so to do by the law, against which thou hast sinned; and therefore for the Lord's sake make haste.

The Third Motive

If they seize upon thee before thou get to the city of Refuge, they will put an everlasting stop to thy journey. This also cries, Run for it.

The Fourth Motive

Know also, that now heaven gates, the heart of Christ, with his arms, are wide open to receive thee. Oh methinks that this consideration, that the devil followeth after to destroy, and that Christ standeth open-armed to receive, should make thee reach out and fly with all haste and speed! And therefore,

The Fifth Motive

Keep thine eye upon the prize; be sure that thy eyes be continually upon the profit thou art like to get. The reason why men are so apt to faint in their race for heaven, it lieth chiefly in either of these two things:

(1) They do not seriously consider the worth of the prize; or else if they do, they are afraid it is too good for them; but most lose heaven for want of considering the price and the worth of it. And therefore, that thou mayest not do the like, keep thine eye much upon the excellency, the sweetness, the beauty, the comfort, the peace, that is to be had there by those that win the prize. This was that which made the apostle run through anything; good report, evil report, persecution, affliction, hunger, nakedness, peril by sea, and peril by land, bonds and imprisonments.

Also it made others endure to be stoned, sawn asunder, to have their eyes bored out with augers, their bodies broiled on gridirons, their tongues cut out of their mouths, boiled in cauldrons, thrown to the wild beasts, burned at the stakes, whipped at posts, and a thousand other fearful torments, 'while they looked not at the things which are seen,' as the things of this world, 'but at the things which are not seen; for the things which are seen are temporal; but the things which are not seen are eternal' (2 Corinthians

4:18). Oh this word 'eternal', that was it that made them, that when they might have had deliverance, they would not accept of it; for they knew in the world to come they should have a better resurrection (Hebrews 11:35).

(2) And do not let the thoughts of the rareness of the place make thee say in thy heart, This is too good for me; for I tell thee, heaven is prepared for whosoever will accept it, and they shall be entertained with hearty good welcome. Consider, therefore, that as bad as thou have got thither; thither went scrubbed, beggarly Lazarus, &c. Nay, it is prepared for the poor: 'Hearken, my beloved brethren,' saith James, take notice of it, 'Hath not God chosen the poor of this world rich in faith, and heirs of the kingdom?' (James 2:5). Therefore take heart and *run*, man. And

The Sixth Motive
Think much of them that are gone before:

First, how really they got into the kingdom.

Secondly, how safe they are in the arms of Jesus; would they be here again for a thousand worlds? Or if they were, would they be afraid that God would not make them welcome?

Thirdly, what would they judge of thee if they knew thy heart began to fail thee in the journey, or thy sins began to allure thee, and to persuade thee to stop thy race? Would they not call thee a thousand fools? and say, Oh, that he did but see what we see, feel what we feel, and taste the dainties that we taste of! Oh, if he were here one quarter of an hour, to behold, to see, to feel, to taste, and enjoy but the thousandth part of what we enjoy, what would he do? What would he suffer? What would he leave undone? Would he favour sin? Would he love this world below? Would he be afraid of friends, or shrink at the most fearful threatenings that the greatest tyrants could invent to give him? Nay, those who have had but a sight of these things by faith, when they have been as far off from them as heaven from earth, yet they have been able to say with a comfortable and merry heart, as the bird that sings in the spring, that this and more shall not keep them from running to heaven.

Sometimes, when my base heart hath been inclining to this world, and to loiter in my journey towards heaven, the very consideration of the glorious saints and angels in heaven, what they enjoy, and what low thoughts they have of the things of this world together, how they would befool me if they did but know what my heart was drawing back; (this) hath caused me to rush forward, to disdain these poor, low, empty, beggarly things, and to say to my soul, Come, soul, let us not be weary; let us see what this heaven is; let us even venture all for it, and try if that will quit the cost.

Surely Abraham, David, Paul, and the rest of the saints of God, were as wise as any are now, and yet they lost all for this glorious kingdom. Oh! therefore, throw away stinking lusts, follow after righteousness, love the Lord Jesus, devote thyself unto his fear, I'll warrant thee he will give thee a goodly recompense. Reader, what sayest thou to this? Art thou resolved to follow me? Nay, resolve if thou canst to get before me. 'So run, that ye may obtain.'

The Seventh Motive

To encourage thee a little farther, set to the work, and when thou hast run thyself down weary, then the Lord Jesus will take thee up, and carry thee. Is not this enough to make any poor soul begin his race? Thou, perhaps, criest, Oh but I am feeble, I am lame, etc., well, but Christ hath a bosom; consider, therefore, when thou hast run thyself down weary, he will put thee in his bosom: 'He shall gather the lambs with his arm and carry them in his bosom, and shall gently lead those that are with young' (Isaiah 40:11). This is the way that fathers take to encourage their children, saying, Run, sweet babe, while thou art weary, and then I will take thee up and carry thee. 'He will gather his lambs with his arm, and carry them in his bosom.' When they are weary they shall ride.

The Eighth Motive

Or else he will convey new strength from heaven into thy soul, which will be as well: 'The youths shall faint and be weary, and the young men shall utterly fall; but they that wait upon the Lord shall renew their strength; they shall mount up with wings as eagles; they shall run and not be weary, they shall walk and not faint' (Isaiah 40:30,31). What shall I say besides what hath already been said? Thou shalt have good easy lodging, good and wholesome diet, the bosom of Christ to lie in, the joys of heaven to feed on. Shall I speak of the satiety and of the duration of all these? Verily to describe them to the height it is a work too hard for me to do.

The Heavenly Footman

The Ninth Motive

Again methinks the very industry of the devil, and the industry of his servants, etc., should make you that have a desire to heaven and happiness to run apace. Why, the devil, he will lose no time, spare no pains, also neither will his servants, both to seek the destruction of themselves and others: and shall not we be as industrious for our own salvation?

Shall the world venture the damnation of their souls for a poor corruptible crown; and shall not we venture the loss of a few trifles for an eternal crown? Shall they venture the loss of eternal friends, as God to love, Christ to redeem, the Holy Spirit to comfort, heaven for habitation, saints and angels for company, and all this to get and hold communion with sin, and this world, and a few base, drunken, swearing, lying, covetous wretches, like themselves?

And shall not we labour as hard, run as fast, seek as diligently, for the company of these glorious eternal friends, though with the loss of such as these, nay, with the loss of ten thousand times better than these poor, low, base, contemptible things? Shall it be said at the last day, that wicked men made more haste to hell than you did make to heaven? That they spent more hours, days, and that early and late, for hell, than you spent for that which is ten thousand thousand of thousands times better? Oh let it not be so, but run with all might and main.

Thus you see I have here spoken something, though but little. Now I shall come to make some use and application of what hath been said, and so conclude.

6. Nine uses of this subject

The first use

You see here, that he that will go to heaven, he must run for it; yea, and not only run, but so run, that is, as I have said, to run earnestly, to run continually, to strip off every thing that would hinder in his race with the rest. Well then, do you so run? And now let us examine a little.

(1) Art thou got into the right way? Art thou in Christ's righteousness? Do not say yes in thy heart, when in truth there is no such matter. It is a dangerous thing, you know, for a man to think he is in the right way, when he is in the wrong. It is the next way for him to lose his way, and not only so, but if he run for heaven, as thou sayest thou dost, even to lose that too. Oh this is the misery of most men, to persuade themselves that they run right, when they never had one foot in the way! The Lord give thee understanding here, or else thou art undone for ever. Prithee, soul, search when was it thou turned out of thy sins and righteousness into the righteousness of Jesus Christ.

I say, dost thou see thyself in him? And is he more precious to thee than the whole world? Is thy mind always musing on him? Dost thou love to be talking of him – and also to be walking with him? Dost thou count his company more precious than the whole world? Dost thou count all things but poor, lifeless, empty, vain things, without communion with him? Doth his company sweeten all things – and his absence embitter all things? Soul, I beseech thee, be serious, and lay it to heart, and do not take things of such weighty concernment as the salvation of damnation of thy soul, without good ground.

(2) Art thou unladen of the things of this world, as pride, pleasures, profits, lusts, vanities? What! Dost thou think to run fast enough with the world, thy sins and lusts in thy heart? I tell thee, soul, they that have laid all aside, every weight, every sin, and are got into the nimblest posture, they find work enough to run; so to run as to hold out. To run through all that opposition, all these jostles, all these rubs, over all these stumbling-blocks, over all the snares from all these entanglements, that the devil, sin, the world, and their own hearts, lay before them; I tell thee, if thou art agoing heavenward, thou wilt find it no small or easy matter. Art thou therefore discharged and unladen of these things? Never talk of going to heaven if thou art not. It is to be feared thou wilt be found among the many that 'will seek to enter in, and shall not be able' (Luke 13:24).

The second use

If so, then, in the next place, what will become of them that are grown weary before they are got half way thither? Why, man, it is he that holdeth out to the end that must be saved; it is he that overcometh that shall inherit all things; it is not every one that begins. Agrippa gave a fair step for a sudden, he steps almost into the bosom of Christ in less than half an hour. 'Thou,' saith he to Paul, hast 'almost persuaded me to be a Christian' (Acts 26:28). Ah! but it was but almost; and so he had as good have been never a whit; he stepped fair indeed, but yet he stepped short; he was hot while he was at it, but he was quickly out of wind. Oh this but almost! I tell you, this but almost, it lost his soul.

Methinks I have seen sometimes how these poor wretches that get but almost to heaven, how fearfully their almost, and their but almost, will torment them in hell; when they shall cry out in the bitterness of their souls, saying, I was almost a Christian, I was almost got into the kingdom, almost out of the hands of the devil, almost out of my sins, almost from under the curse of God; almost, and that was all; almost, but not altogether. Oh that I should be almost at heaven, and should not go quite through!

Friend, it is a sad thing to sit down before we are in heaven, and to grow weary before we come to the place of rest; and if it should be thy case, I am sure thou dost not so run as to obtain. But again,

The third use

In the next place, What then will become of them that some time since were running post-haste to heaven, insomuch that they seemed to outstrip many, but now are running as fast back again? Do you think those will ever come thither? What, to run back again, back again to sin, to the world, to the devil, back again to the lusts of the flesh? Oh! 'It had been better for them not to have known the way of righteousness, than after they had known it, to turn,' to turn back again, 'from the holy commandment' (2 Peter 2:21).

Those men shall not only be damned for sin, but for

professing to all the world that sin is better than Christ; for the man that runs back again, he doth as good as say, 'I have tried Christ, and I have tried sin, and I do not find so much profit in Christ as in sin.' I say, this man declareth this, even by his running back again.

Oh sad! What a doom they will have, who were almost at heaven's gates, and then run back again. 'If any draw back,' saith Christ (by his apostle), 'my soul shall have no pleasure in him' (Hebrews 10:38). Again, 'No man having put his hand to the plough,' that is, set forward, in the ways of God, 'and looking back,' turning back again, 'is fit for the kingdom of God' (Luke 9:62).

And if not fit for the kingdom of heaven then for certain he must needs be fit for the fire of hell. And therefore, saith the apostle, those that 'bring forth' these apostatising fruits, as 'briars and thorns, are rejected, and nigh unto cursing, whose end is to be burned' (Hebrews 6:8). Oh there is never another Christ to save them by bleeding and dying for them! And if they shall not escape that neglect, then how shall they escape that reject and turn their back upon 'so great a salvation' (Hebrews 2:3)? If the righteous, that is, they that run for it, will find work enough to get to heaven, then where will the 'ungodly', backsliding 'sinner appear?' Or if Judas, the traitor, or Francis Spira the backslider, were but now alive in the world to whisper these men in the ear a little, and tell them what it hath cost their souls for backsliding, surely it would stick by them and make them afraid of running back again, so long as they had one day to live in this world.

The fourth use

So again, fourthly, how unlike to these men's passions will those be that have all this while sat still, and have not so much as set one foot forward to the kingdom of heaven. Surely he that backslides, and he that sitteth still in sin, they are both of one mind; the one he will not stir, because he loveth his sins, and the things of this world; the other he runs back again, because he loveth his sins, and the things of this world; is it not one and the same thing? They are all one here, and shall not one and the same hell hold them hereafter! He is an ungodly one that never looked after Christ, and he is an ungodly one that did once look after him and then ran quite back again; and therefore that word must certainly drop out of the mouth of Christ against them both, 'Depart from me, ye cursed, into everlasting fire, prepared for the devil and his angels' (Matthew 25:41).

The fifth use

Again, here you may see, in the next place, that is, they that will have heaven must run for it; then this calls aloud to those who began but a while since to run, I say, for them to mend their pace if they intend to win; you know that they which come hindmost, had need run fastest.

Friend, I tell thee, there be those that have run ten years to thy one, nay, twenty to thy five, and yet if thou talk with them, sometimes they will say they doubt they shall come late enough. How then will it be with thee? Look to it therefore that thou delay no time, not an hour's time, but speedily part with all, with everything that is an hindrance to thee in thy journey, and run; yea, and so run that thou mayest obtain.

The sixth use

Again, sixthly, You that are old professors, take you heed that the young striplings of Jesus, that began to strip but the other day, do not outrun you, so as to have that scripture fulfilled on you, 'The first shall be last, and the last first'; which will be a shame to you, and a credit for them. What, for a young soldier to be more courageous than he that hath been used to wars! To you that are hindmost, I say, strive to outrun them that are before you; and you that are foremost, I say, hold your ground, and keep before them in faith and love, if possible; for indeed that is the right running, for one to strive to outrun another; even for the hindmost to endeavour to overtake the foremost, and he that is before should be sure to lay out himself to keep his ground, even to the very utmost. But then,

The seventh use

Again, how basely do they behave themselves, how unlike are they to win, that think it enough to keep company with the hindmost? There are some men that profess themselves such as run for heaven as well as any; yet if there be but any lazy, slothful, cold, half-hearted professors in the country, they will be sure to take example by them; they think if they can but keep pace with them they shall do fair; but these do not consider that the hindmost lose the prize.

You may know it, if you will, that it cost the foolish virgins dear for their coming too late: 'They that were ready went in with him, and the door was shut. Afterward,' mark, 'afterward came the other,' the foolish, 'virgins, saying, "Lord, Lord, open to us"; but he answered, and said, "Depart, I know you not"' (Matthew 25:10-12). Depart, lazy professors, cold professors, slothful professors.

Oh! methinks the Word of God is so plain for the overthrow of your lazy professors, that it is to be wondered men do take no more notice of it. How was Lot's wife served for running lazily, and for giving but one look behind her, after the things she left in Sodom? How was Esau served for staying too long before he came for the blessing? And how were they served that are mentioned in the thirteenth of Luke, 'for staying till the door was shut?' Also the foolish virgins; a heavy after-groan will they give that have thus stayed too long. It turned Lot's wife into a pillar of salt (Genesis 19:26). It made Esau weep with an exceeding loud and bitter cry (Hebrews 12:17). It made Judas hang himself; yea, and it will make thee curse the day in which thou wast born, if thou miss of the kingdom, as thou wilt certainly do, if this be thy course. But,

The eighth use

Again, how, and if thou by thy lazy running shouldst not only destroy thyself, but also thereby be the cause of the damnation of some other, for thou being a professor thou must think that others will take notice of thee: and because thou art but a poor, cold, lazy runner, and one that seeks to drive the world and pleasures along with thee: why, thereby, others will think of doing so too. Nay, say they, why may not we as well as he?

He is a professor, and yet he seeks for pleasures, riches, profits; he loveth vain company, and he is proud, and he is so and so, and professes that he is going for heaven; yea, and he saith also he doth not fear but he shall have entertainment; let us therefore keep pace with him, we shall fare no worse than he. Oh how fearful a thing will it be, if that thou shalt be instrumental of the ruin of others by thy halting in the way of righteousness!

Look to it, thou wilt have strength little enough to appear before God, to give an account of the loss of thy own soul; thou needest not have to give an account for others; why, thou didst stop them from entering in. How wilt thou answer that saying, You would not enter in yourselves, and them that would you hinder: for that saying will be eminently fulfilled on them that through their own idleness do keep themselves out of heaven, and by giving of others the same example, hinder them also.

The ninth use
Therefore, now to speak a word to both of you, and so I shall conclude.

(1) I beseech you, in the name of our Lord Jesus Christ, that none of you do run so lazily in the way to heaven as to hinder either yourselves or others. I know that even he which runs laziest, if he should see a man running for a temporal life, if he should so much neglect

his own well-being in this world as to venture, when he is a-running for his life, to pick up here and there a lock of wool that hangeth by the wayside, or to step now and then aside out of the way to gather up a straw or two, or any rotten stick, I say, if he should do this when he is a-running for his life, thou wouldst condemn him; and dost thou not condemn thyself that dost the very same in effect, nay worse, that loiterest in thy race, notwithstanding thy soul, heaven, glory, and all is at stake. Have a care, have a care, poor wretched sinner, have a care!

(2) If yet there shall be any that, notwithstanding this advice, will still be flaggering and loitering in the way to the kingdom of glory, be thou so wise as not to take example by them. Learn of no man further than he followeth Christ. But look unto Jesus, who is not only 'the author and finisher of faith,' but who did, 'for the joy that was set before him, endured the cross, despising the shame, and is now set down at the right hand of God' (Hebrews 12:2).

I say, look to no man to learn of him, no further than he followeth Christ. 'Be ye followers of me,' saith Paul, 'even as I also am of Christ' (1 Corinthians 11:1). Though he was an eminent man, yet his exhortation was, that none should follow him any further than he followed Christ.

7. Provocation (to run with the foremost)

Now that you may be provoked to run with the foremost, take notice of this. When Lot and his wife were running from cursed Sodom to the mountains, to save their lives, it is said that his wife looked back from behind him, and she became a pillar of salt; and yet you see that neither her practice, nor the judgment of God that fell upon her for the same, would cause Lot to look behind him. I have sometimes wondered at Lot in this particular; his wife looked behind her, and died immediately, but let what would become of her, Lot would not so much as look behind him to see her. We do not read that he did so much as once look where she was, or what was become of her; his heart was indeed upon his journey, and well it might; there was the mountain before him, and the fire and brimstone behind him; his life lay at stake, and he had lost it if he had but looked behind him. Do thou so run: and in thy race remember Lot's wife, and remember her doom; and remember for what that doom did overtake her; and remember that God made her an example for all lazy runners, to the end of the world: and take heed thou fall not after the same example. But, if this will not provoke thee, consider thus,

1. Thy soul is thy own soul, that is either to be saved or lost; thou shalt not lose my soul by thy laziness. It is thy own soul, thy own ease, thy own peace, thy own advantage, or disadvantage. If it were my soul that thou art desired to be good unto, methinks reason should move thee somewhat to pity it. But alas, it is thy own, thy own soul. 'What shall it profit a man if he shall gain the whole world, and lose his own soul?' (Mark 8:36). God's people wish well to the souls of others, and wilt not thou wish well to thy own? And if this will not provoke thee, then think again,

2. If thou lose thy soul, it is thou also that must bear the blame. It made Cain stark mad to consider that he had

not looked to his brother Abel's soul. How much more will it perplex thee to think, that thou hadst not a care of thy own? And if this will not provoke thee to bestir thyself, think again,

3. That if thou wilt not run, the people of God are resolved to deal with thee even as Lot dealt with his wife, that is, leave thee behind them. It may be thou hast a father, mother, brother, etc., going post-haste to heaven, wouldst thou be willing to be left behind them? Surely no. Again,

4. Will it not be a dishonour to thee to see the very boys and girls in the country to have more wit than thyself? It may be the servants of some men, as the horsekeeper, ploughman, scullion, are more looking after heaven than their masters. I am apt to think sometimes, that more servants than masters, that more tenants than landlords, will inherit the kingdom of heaven. But is not this a shame for them that are such? I am persuaded you scorn, that your servants should say that they are wiser than you in the things of this world; and yet I am bold to say, that many of them are wiser than you in the things of the world to come, which are of greater concernment.

8. A short expostulation

Well, then, sinner, what sayest thou? Where is thy heart? Wilt thou run? Art thou resolved to strip? Or art thou not? Think quickly, man, it is no dallying in this matter. Confer not with flesh and blood; look up to heaven, and see how thou likest it; also to hell – of which thou mayest understand something by my book, called, *A Few Sighs from Hell; or the Groans of a Damned Soul*; which I wish thee to read seriously over — and accordingly devote thyself. If thou dost not know the way, inquire at the Word of God. If thou wantest company, cry for God's Spirit. If thou wantest encouragement, entertain the promises. But be sure thou begin by times; get into the way; run apace and hold out to the end; and the Lord give thee a prosperous journey. Farewell.

—— Other books —— of Interest by Christian Focus

******

The Holy War

Complete and Unabridged Edition
John Bunyan

'In the Holy War John Bunyan sets about creating nothing less than an epic. In this richly inventive book Bunyan points up allegorical truths about the Christian life and the history of the church.'
Dr Tim Dowley

The Holy War is a fascinating gripping book. Its plot is involving and colourful. Like the best of the ancient sagas we are enthralled by how the tale is told.

The language of the narrative is racy, inventive, often humorous and always communicating directly with ordinary people in the vocabulary of common speech... seventeenth century England lives again in these pages.

David Porter

Born in 1628, the son of a tinker, John Bunyan suffered persecution and imprisonment under Charles II. During this time he wrote five epic works which have made him one of the world's most famous and enduring writers.

ISBN 1 85792 0287

Puritan Profiles

54 Members and Contemporaries of the
Westminster Assembly
William Barker

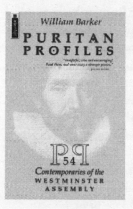

'*...insightful, wise and encouraging! Read them, and come away a stronger person.*'

James Boice,
Tenth Presbyterian Church,
Philadelphia

'*Will Barker's love of biography, historian's eye for detail, his personal devotion to Christ and Scripture make these pages an expertly guided tour of the varied characters and remarkable personalities drawn together by the Westminster Assembly*'.

Sinclair Ferguson,
Tron Kirk, Glasgow

William Barker is vice-president for academic affairs and Professor of Church History at Westminster Theological Seminary, Philadelphia. He is an ordained minister in the Presbyterian Church in America, of which he is a former moderator. His keen interest in contemporary culture and politics ensures that this book is relevant today.

ISBN 1 85792 191 7

The Intercession of Christ

A Puritan's View of Christ's mediating work
John Bunyan
Introduced by William Barker

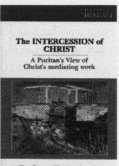

John Bunyan has been called the most influential of the Puritans but whilst it is true to say that his books have sold more than any other writer of his era, at the time he wrote them he was a largely unknown itinerant preacher / tinker. Pilgrim's Progress was only published after John Owen gave his recommendation to the printer!

Bunyan has a brilliant ability to tell a story with deep theological roots in which you recognise yourself. His allegories convey Christian truth to those without a theological background in a way, perhaps, only matched by C.S. Lewis in a later era.

In The Intercession of Christ Bunyan traces the nature of Jesus' intercession, who it should affect, the benefits it gives us and how effective that intercession is. Bunyan is also keen to show the inferences of the doctrine on such subjects as backsliding, how Christ's intervention is affected when we continue to sin, and are the sins of God's people worse than the sins of others?

ISBN 1 85792 4126

The Mortification of Sin

A Puritan's View on how to Deal with Sin in your Life
John Owen
Introduced by J.I. Packer

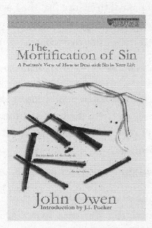

'I owe more to John Owen than to any other theologian, ancient or modern, and I owe more to this little book than to anything else he wrote.'
J.I. Packer

John Owen insisted on the importance of Christians dealing effectively with their sinful tendencies and attitudes. He believed that God, through his Word and Spirit, had provided the guidelines and the power for this to be achieved.

In this book, John Owen effectively dismisses various excuses for not engaging in self-scrutiny and yet avoids the current trend of self-absorption. In so doing he provides principles to help believers live lives of holiness.

J I Packer, one of the best-known contemporary writers and theologians who re-introduced the Puritans to the modern church, provides a fascinating introduction.

ISBN 1 85792 1070

Christian Focus Publications

publishes books for all ages

Our mission statement -
STAYING FAITHFUL
In dependence upon God we seek to help make his infallible
word, the Bible, relevant. Our aim is to ensure that the Lord
Jesus Christ is presented as the only hope to obtain forgiveness
of sin, live a useful life and look forward to heaven with him.

REACHING OUT
Christ's last command requires us to reach out to our world
with his gospel. We seek to help fulfil that by publishing books
that point people towards Jesus and help them to develop a
Christ-like maturity. We aim to equip all levels of readers for
life, work ministry and mission.

Books in our adult range are published in three imprints.

Christian Focus contains popular works including biographies,
commentaries, basic doctrine, and Christian living. Our
children's books are also published in this imprint.
Mentor focuses on books written at a level suitable for Bible
College and seminary students, pastors, and other serious
readers; the imprint includes commentaries, doctrinal stud-
ies, examination of current issues, and church history.
Christian Heritage contains classic writings from the past.

For a free catalogue of all our titles, please write to:
Christian Focus Publications, Ltd
Geanies House, Fearn,
Ross-shire, IV20 1TW, Scotland, United Kingdom
info@christianfocus.com

For details of our titles visit us on our website
www.christianfocus.com